Washed Away!

Story by Dawn McMillan

Illustrated by Liz Alger

Rigby PM Plus Chapter Books
part of the Rigby PM Program
Emerald Level

U.S. edition © 2003 Rigby Education
Harcourt Achieve Inc.
10801 N. MoPac Expressway
Building #3
Austin, TX 78759
www.harcourtachieve.com

Text © 2003 Thomson Learning Australia
Illustrations © 2003 Thomson Learning Australia
Originally published in Australia by Thomson Learning Australia

10 9 8 7 6 5 4 3
07 06

Washed Away!
    ISBN 0 7578 4117 1

Printed in China by 1010 Printing International Ltd

Contents

Chapter 1

Ready to Go

It looks as if we're going to be flooded out! I'm a bit scared but I'm trying not to show it. Dad has enough to worry about and I don't want him to worry about me, too. I think he does though, because he pats me on the shoulder every time he passes. I know Dad will look after me, and I'm going to look after him!

We've got everything ready. We can only take a few things, and some warm clothes and a spare jacket. I'm taking my photo of Mom, my toothbrush, my sleeping bag, and my spare sneakers. Dad says we'll need some dry shoes for when we get to the rescue center. We'll have to walk in the water to launch our boat. The boat looks really strange sitting in the middle of our lawn. It's tied to the porch post so if the flood water comes up quickly, it won't float away.

I'm worried about leaving our house. My room's upstairs so that's not so bad, but downstairs we've had to put lots of things up high. Our photos and our important papers are up in the attic! The television and our books are on the table. So is the CD player. I helped Dad roll up our rugs and they are on the window seat. It was fun at the time, like an adventure, but now it doesn't feel so good. I don't want our house ruined by dirty flood water.

I'm *really* worried about William. Dad and I both love William. When we watch television at night, he sits between us and we scratch his ears. He likes that. I've put lots of dry cat food and a container of fresh water on the bench for him. I don't want to leave him, but I know he's better off here than being kept in a box. He's here beside me, fast asleep…

Dad's back from putting the car up on the high part of our yard. I can hear the emergency sirens wailing, over and over, and the water is at the end of our street. I have to go and help Dad. We really *are* going to evacuate! I'm taking my journal so I'll write some more later. Good-bye, house! Good-bye, William!

Chapter 2

Cat Overboard!

I think William has drowned, and it's all my fault! I shouldn't have done it, but I couldn't bear to leave him.

Dad was telling me to hurry. He was racing around turning off the electricity and the gas and collecting our survival kit. I picked up my bag and followed him out to the porch. He threw me my life jacket and told me to get it on, but I just couldn't leave William.

I raced back inside and put William in my bag. He looked very surprised as I closed the zipper quickly and ran outside. The water was already through the hedge. I put my bag, and William, into the boat. We pushed the boat into the flood water, then stepped in. Dad started the motor and suddenly there was a howl from inside my bag. William pushed against the zipper and it opened slowly. I saw his bright yellow eyes blazing and his fur standing straight up as he came out through the top of the bag.

Dad yelled, "You've got the cat!"

William leaped onto the edge of the boat. I jumped up to grab him but Dad shouted, "Sit down! You'll have us all in the water!"

Then William lost his balance and he was gone.

I screamed as I saw him disappear in the dirty water.

"Please turn around, Dad!" I yelled. "Please!"

Dad shook his head.

"I can't do that, Nicholas," he said. "We both love William but you are the most important thing to me. I need to get you to safety."

I cried and cried, and Dad cried a little bit too.

Dad keeps telling me that William will be all right.

"Cats can swim, Nicholas," he says, "and he wasn't far from dry land."

I want to believe him but a little voice inside me tells me that William is dead. Dad's been looking after me all day, but now he's gone to make sandbags. I wish I could have gone with him, but he says I can help in the morning.

I guess it's okay in this hall. Our friend, Mrs. McGregor, has been looking after everyone. Now she and Mr. McGregor are cooking hot dogs on a portable gas stove. I'll have a hot dog, then I'll crawl into my sleeping bag. If I go to sleep I won't have to think about William.

Chapter 3

Race Against the River

I woke up when Dad came back last night. He said the river was still rising, but it was his turn to rest. I pulled my sleeping bag close to his, and we drifted off to sleep.

This morning we got up early, and Mrs. McGregor was cooking breakfast. There were two big pots of oatmeal bubbling on the gas stove, and lots of buttered toast.

I wanted to go straight to work, but Dad said, "You can't do a day's hard labor on an empty stomach, young man!" and he ruffled my hair.

We went down to the river bank in Mr. McGregor's four-wheel-drive. It was scary down there. The water was thick and brown, and tree trunks and clumps of grass rushed past. At the bridge, there were logs jammed against the piles.

"Come on, Nicholas!" Dad called. "No time to waste! If the water comes over here it'll go right through the school."

I raced over to where a big pile of sand had been dumped, and helped to fill the bags. Dad and the other people carried the heavy sandbags to the bank, to make a wall.

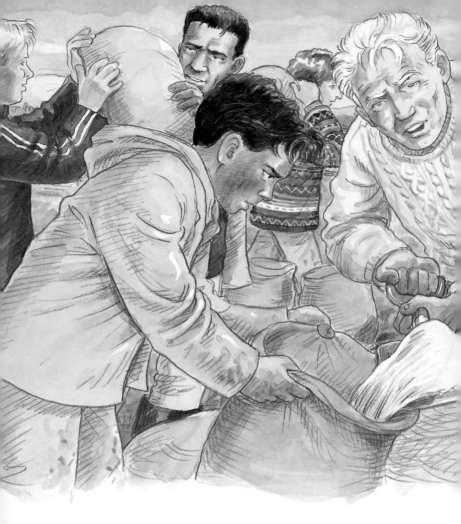

The water kept rising. It was racing us, teasing us. We kept on shoveling and building the wall, and just as we ran out of sand, the water came no further. I sat down and looked at my hands. My palms stung and I felt like crying.

Dad came and sat down beside me. He put his arm around my shoulders and pulled me to him.

"I'm proud of you, Nicholas," he said.

I looked up at his dirty face. I was proud of him, too.

We were hungry when we got back to the hall, and dirty and wet. Just as well we had spare clothes. After I'd changed, Mrs. McGregor cooked me more hot dogs. I love hot dogs!

I can't write any more tonight. My hands are too sore and my whole body aches. I wish I could have a hot shower but there are no showers here, and no electricity. It's a good rescue center though. It has all the things we need, like toilets, and cooking pots, and plates and cups.

It's stopped raining. The announcer on the radio says the worst is over. Tomorrow we might be able to go home. I hope I find William!

Chapter 4

Home Again

What a day! I've got so much to write about! I'm in my own bed tonight. It's so good to be home. We still have no electricity so I'm writing by flashlight. I'll need our spare batteries soon. Dad has just brought me some hot chocolate. Just as well we left a bucket of fresh water on the bench before we left home. It wouldn't be safe to drink the tap water right now. And it's lucky we have a gas stove too, or I'd be drinking *cold* chocolate. Yuck!

We came home this afternoon. Some people had to stay at the rescue center for another night, but we were lucky because the water went down quickly in our part of town. We walked home. Dad laughed about the boat not being much use without any water. I laughed with him, but part of me wanted to cry. I was afraid to go home because I might not find William. Dad knew I was worried so he told lots of jokes. I think he was trying to take my mind off William.

21

We didn't joke much when we got to the main part of town.

Dad said, "Here, Nicholas, walk along the middle of the road where it's highest. Keep away from that deep mud. You never know what might be under there."

The stores were such a mess! Everyone was sweeping the mud and water out the doors, and there was soaked, dirty stuff piled everywhere.

Lots of houses were ruined. Poor Mr. and Mrs. Jacobsen! The flood took a whole wall away from their house, and their kitchen table was out in the middle of the yard. Mrs. Jacobsen was crying, and Mr. Jacobsen just shook his head when we tried to talk to him.

Mr. Roscoe was really brave.

"It could be worse!" he called out to us, but I didn't think it could be much worse for him. His car was covered in mud, and the water was still in his house.

We walked around the corner and up to our house. My heart was pounding. I moved closer to Dad and I thought I could hear his heart pounding, too. We stopped at the gate. The front walk was covered in mud, and we could see the water mark above the porch.

Dad was very quiet.

"It got in!" was all he said.

We opened the door and saw the streaks of mud lying where the water had been.

"It's just the kitchen and bathroom, Dad," I said, trying to make him feel better.

"You're right, Nicholas," he replied. "We're lucky!"

Then Dad looked serious. "We have something really important to do," he whispered. I knew what he meant. We had to find William!

Chapter 5

Looking for William

We looked all around the yard for William, under the hedge and in the shrubs.

"He could be under the house," said Dad. "I'll check it out."

I was worried about William being trapped under the house. Dad read my thoughts.

"The water didn't reach this corner," he said. "He could be under there, Nicholas."

When Dad came out from under the house, his pants were wet with mud.

"No William," he said softly, and I felt the tears sting my eyes.

There didn't seem to be anywhere else to look. Dad held me close. "We'll just have to wait," he said. "William might come home."

I sat on the damp porch and watched Dad go up to get the car. I kept thinking that William was sitting on the railing behind me but when I turned my head I knew I was imagining it. Everything seemed so quiet.

Then I heard Dad's voice. "Nicholas! Come here! Quickly!"

I ran up to the car, wondering what was wrong. Dad was standing by the driver's door.

"I forgot to put the window up," he laughed. "We've got a wet car, but guess what else we've got!"

I peered into the car. There, curled up in a small muddy ball, was William!

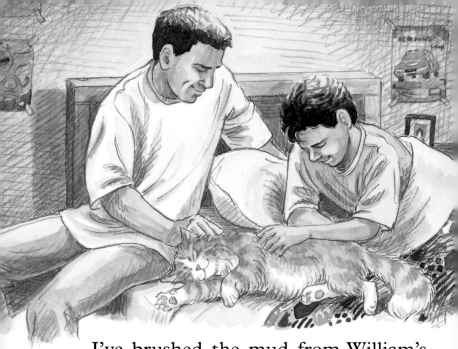

I've brushed the mud from William's fur, and now he's here beside me sleeping soundly. I guess he's tired from all that swimming. And Dad's sitting on my bed, scratching William's ears.

Tomorrow Dad and I will pull up the kitchen and bathroom floor tile. We'll be busy cleaning and drying out our rooms. I don't think William will be much help. He'll just sit on the porch railing and watch us work.